What Huskies Love a

What Huskies Love and Respect About Cougars

What Huskies Love and Respect About Cougars

What Huskies Love and Respect About Cougars

What Huskies Love and Respect About Cougars

What Huskies Love and Respect About Cougars

What Huskies Love and Respect About Cougars

What Huskies Love and Respect About Cougars

What Huskies Love and Respect About Cougars

What Huskies Love and Respect About Cougars

2

What Huskies Love and Respect About Cougars

23

What Huskies Love and Respect About Cougars

What Huskies Love and Respect About Cougars

What Huskies Love and Respect About Cougars

What Huskies Love and Respect About Cougars

What Huskies Love and Respect About Cougars

What Huskies Love and Respect About Cougars

What Huskies Love and Respect About Cougars

What Huskies Love and Respect About Cougars

What Huskies Love and Respect About Cougars

What Huskies Love and Respect About Cougars

What Huskies Love and Respect About Cougars

What Huskies Love and Respect About Cougars

What Huskies Love and Respect About Cougars

What Huskies Love and Respect About Cougars

What Huskies Love and Respect About Cougars

What Huskies Love and Respect About Cougars

What Huskies Love and Respect About Cougars

What Huskies Love and Respect About Cougars

What Huskies Love and Respect About Cougars

What Huskies Love and Respect About Cougars

126

What Huskies Love and Respect About Cougars

What Huskies Love and Respect About Cougars

What Huskies Love and Respect About Cougars

Made in United States
Troutdale, OR
03/31/2025